Hello AMBULANCE

MOLLY PERFORMS CPR

In loving memory of
Betty Pennington.

**Amazing mum to three beautiful children;
Alba, Iona, and Hamish.**

Paramedic, loving wife and friend.

A gentle, honest soul. She is truly missed.

Let's live to be her legacy.

Be your best. Be more Betty.

❤️

Just down the road, not too far away,

Mollie was staying with her favourite Aunt May.

Breakfast was yummy; Mollie wanted more,

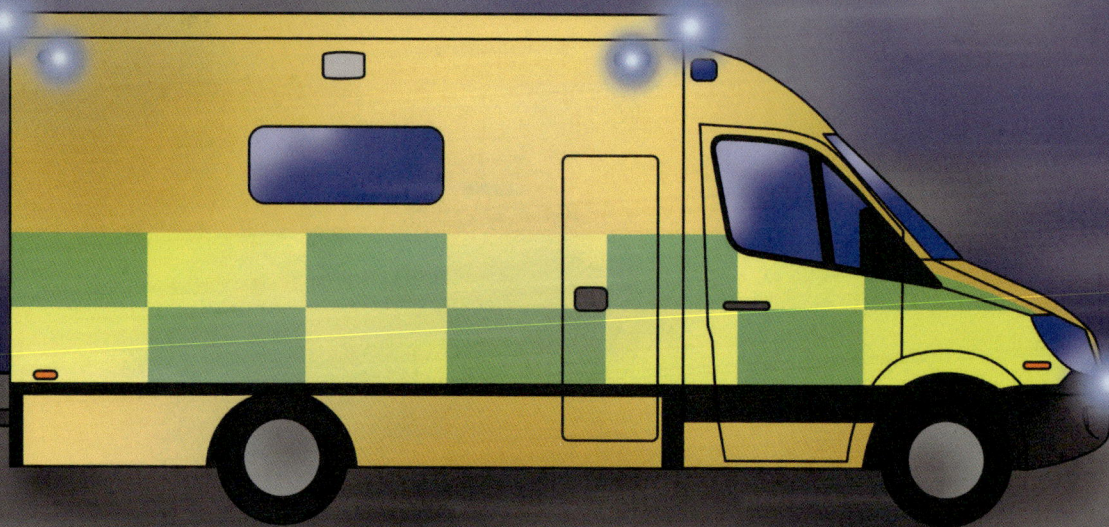

"If the answer is no, we must do CPR. The ambulance is coming. We know where you are."

"Unlock the front door," the call taker said.
"Lay Aunty flat and tilt back her head."

"Push down on her chest, hard and fast."
Mollie remembered she'd learned this in class.

Paramedic Pip and EMT Tom, were on their way, their sirens on.

"CPR is in progress," read Pip on the screen.
"The caller is 7, let's hurry to the scene."

Rapid Response Rhian arrived with the crew. They grabbed their equipment as Mollie's Mum arrived too.

Inside they found Mollie pushing down on Aunty's chest. Tom radioed control. "Confirmed, cardiac arrest."

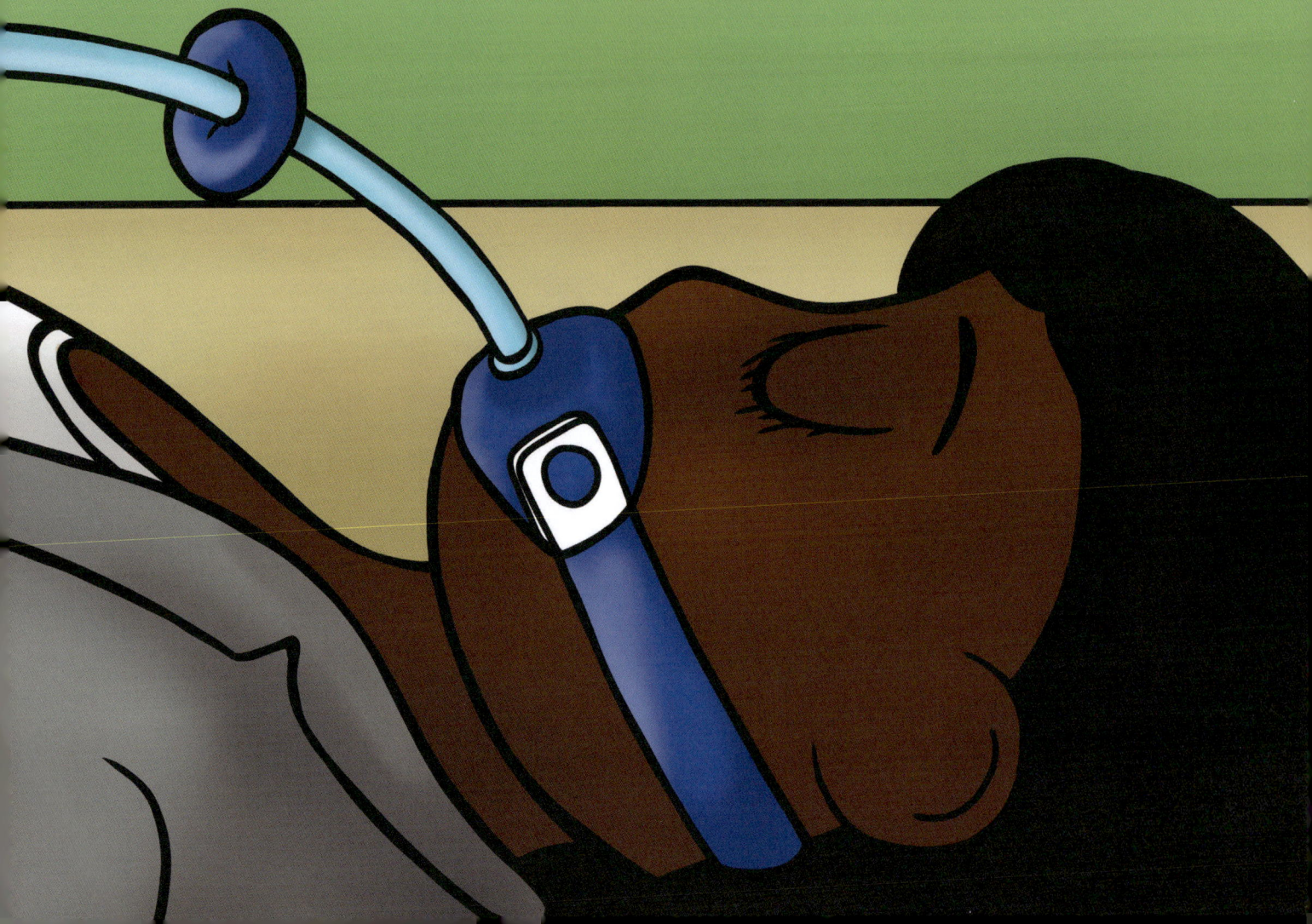

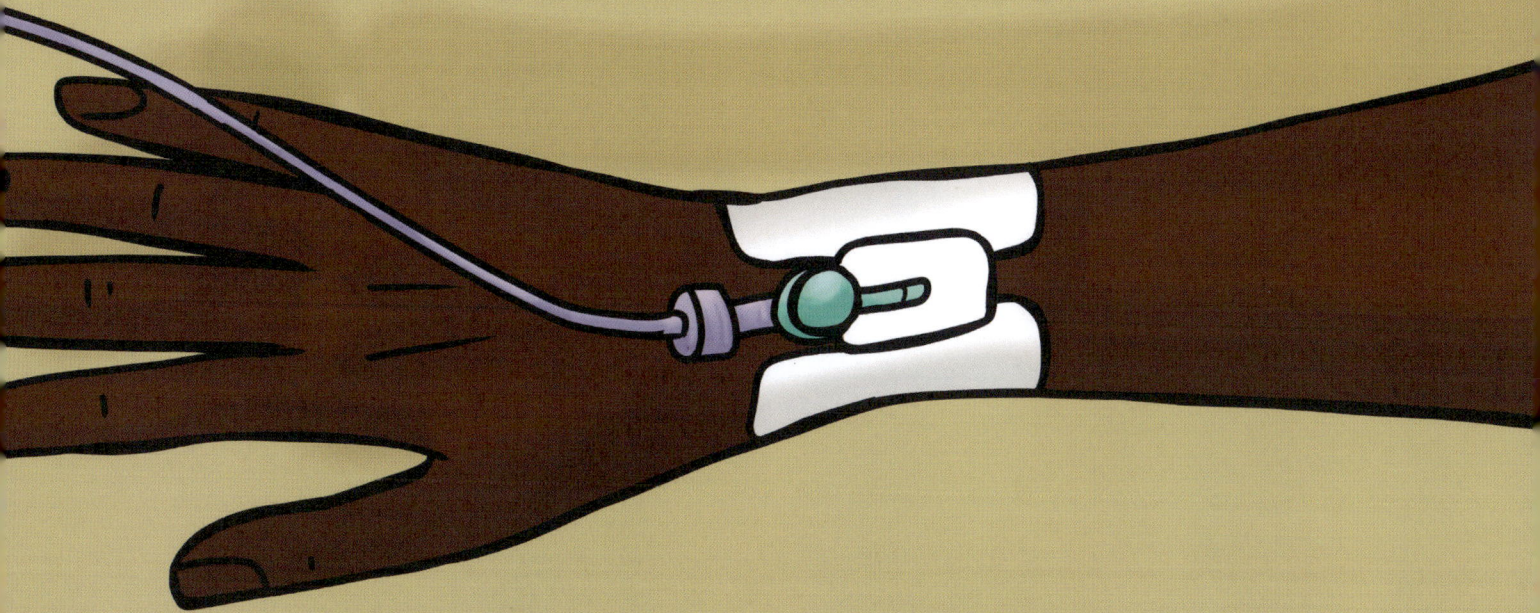

A tube in Aunty's mouth, a needle in her arm.
A lot going on, but everyone calm.

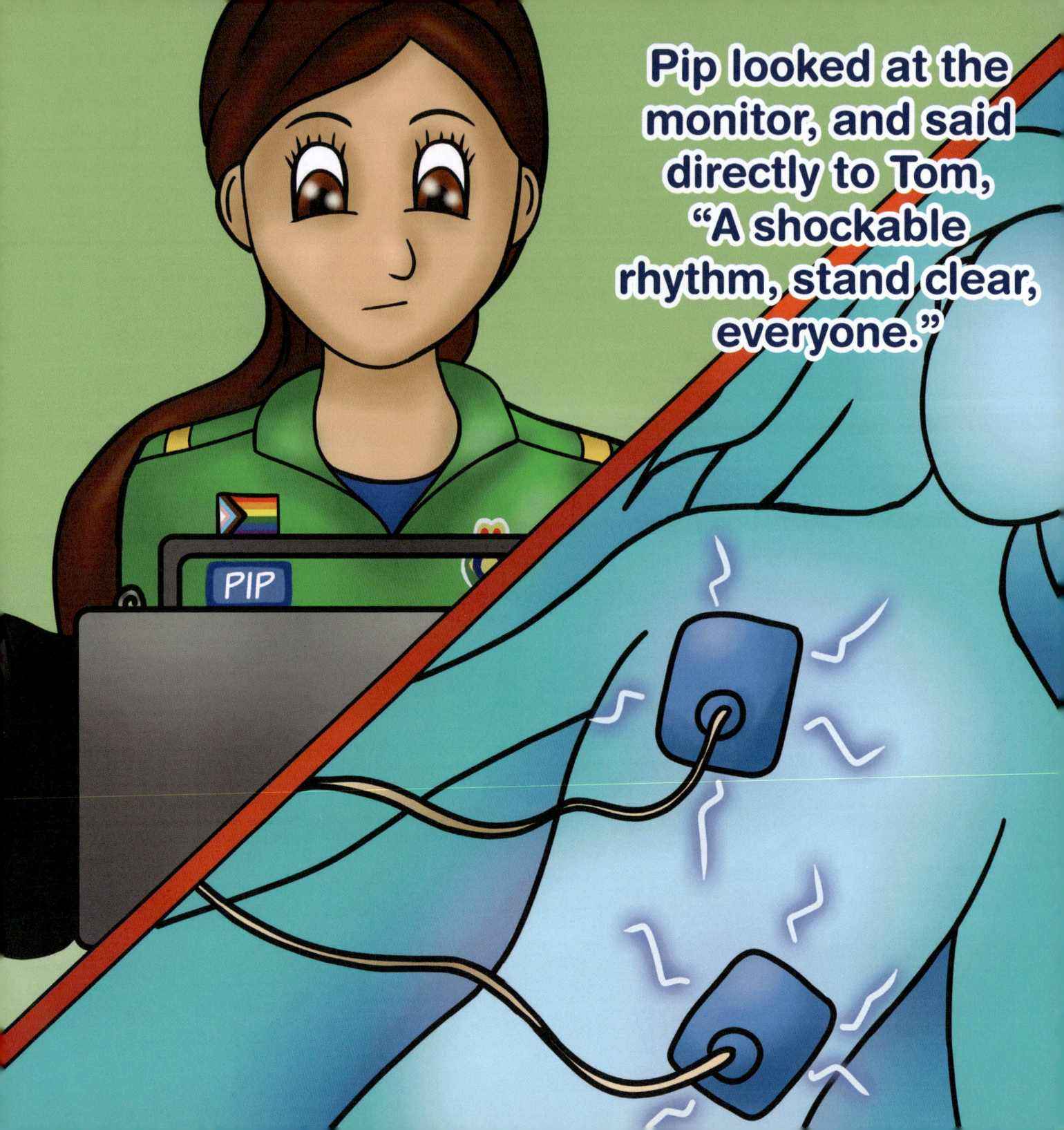

Pip looked at the monitor, and said directly to Tom, "A shockable rhythm, stand clear, everyone."

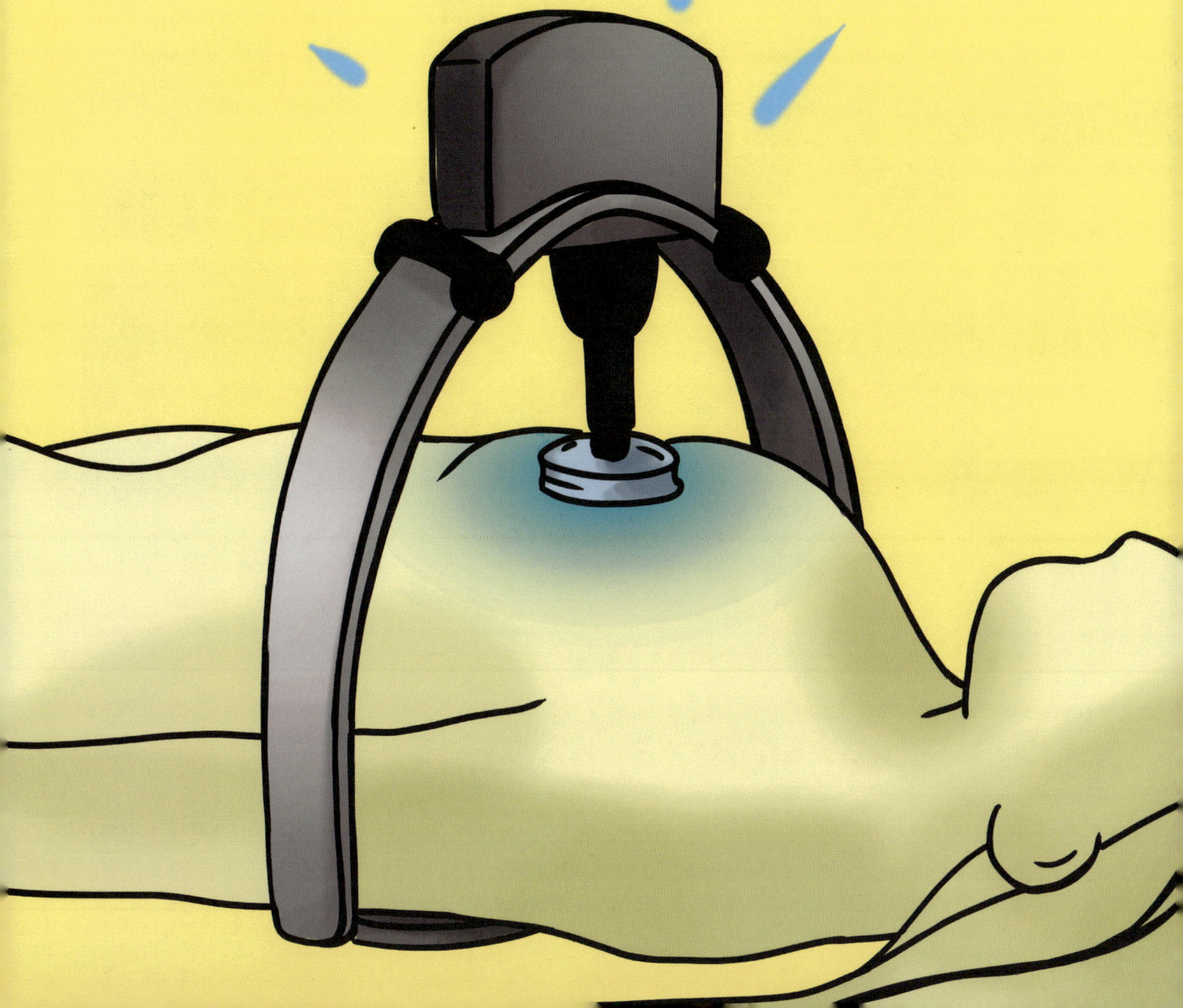

A noisy machine now pumping her chest.
All working hard, wishing for the best.

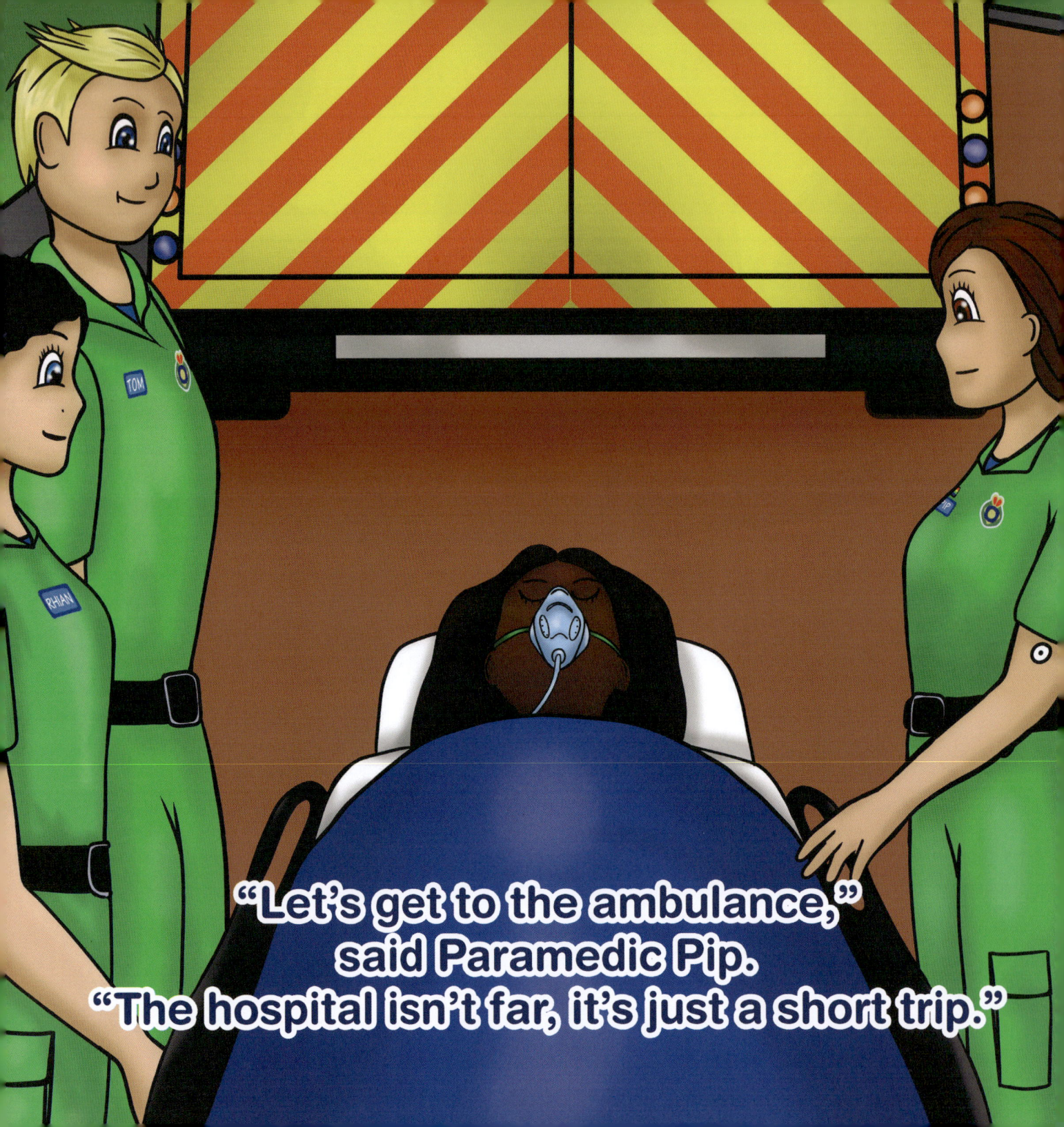

"Let's get to the ambulance,"
said Paramedic Pip.
"The hospital isn't far, it's just a short trip."

Mollie with her mum,
the crew ready to go.
Rhian turned to Tom.
"Look, another young hero."

LIFE SUPPORT INSTRUCTIONS

- Is the patient breathing?
- Can you see their chest rise and fall?
- Shout for help.
- Call 999!
- Ask for an ambulance and tell them your location.
- Listen carefully to what the call taker has to say.
- Basic life support instructions will be given.
- Follow them as best as you can.
- Try to stay calm.
  Help is on the way.

Printed in Great Britain
by Amazon